P9-AFB-944

An Anthology of Piano Music Volume II

The Classical Period

**Selected and Edited
by Denes Agay**

**With an Introduction
by Louis L. Crowder**

Head of the Department of Music
The University of Connecticut

Yorktown Music Press
New York/London/Sydney

Riverside Community College
Library
OCT '98
4800 Magnolia Avenue
Riverside, CA 92506

M 21 .A225 A6 1971 v.2

An Anthology of piano music

Copyright © 1971 Yorktown Music Press, Inc.

All rights reserved. No part of this book may be
reproduced in any form or by any electronic or mechanical means
including information storage and retrieval systems,
without permission in writing from the publisher
except by a reviewer who may quote brief passages in a review.

Order No. YK 20220
International Standard Book Number: 0.8256.8042.5
Library of Congress Catalog Card Number: 72-150252

Exclusive Distributors:
Music Sales Corporation
257 Park Avenue South, New York, NY 10010 USA
Music Sales Limited
8/9 Frith Street, London W1V 5TZ England
Music Sales Pty. Limited
120 Rothschild Street, Rosebery, Sydney, NSW 2018, Australia

Printed in the United States of America by
Vicks Lithograph and Printing Corporation

FOREWORD

The content of AN ANTHOLOGY OF PIANO MUSIC was selected from the keyboard literature of nearly four centuries. From the early Baroque to the present, through the works of 139 composers, all important musical idioms and modes of expression are represented. The material is divided into four volumes:

Volume I —THE BAROQUE PERIOD — from the end of the 16th century (late Renaissance) to the end of the 18th (Rococo).

Volume II —THE CLASSICAL PERIOD — the second half of the 18th and the early 19th centuries. (Haydn, Mozart, Beethoven and their contemporaries.)

Volume III —THE ROMANTIC PERIOD — piano music of the 19th century.

Volume IV —THE TWENTIETH CENTURY — piano works by major composers of our time.

It is hardly necessary to point out that no rigid stylistic boundaries separate these volumes and that, inevitably, there is some chronological and idiomatic overlapping. The works of the sons of Johann Sebastian Bach, for instance, which conclude the baroque volume could have been placed as well at the beginning of the classical section. Fauré, Sibelius, Rachmaninoff and others, who wrote during the late 19th and early 20th centuries, could have been included in either the romantic or the contemporary volume, depending on whether we consider their modes of writing or their life-spans as a yardstick. It is better, then, to view this Anthology, and for that matter, the entire music literature, not as a succession of clearly separated and defined plateaus, but rather as a broad, ever-flowing stream with many branches and tributaries. This stream, the literature of keyboard music, is so vast that even the impressively sizable body of this Anthology, amounting to nearly one thousand pages, can represent but a small fraction of it.

This fact alone can give a hint of the difficult process involved in selecting the contents of these volumes and of the often thorny decisions the editor had to make. Which Preludes and Fugues of Bach's "48" should be chosen? Which Sonatas of Mozart and Beethoven should be included? Are the contributions to keyboard romanticism of an Heller or an Alkan substantial enough to warrant inclusion? Is the amount of space allocated to a certain composer in proper ratio to his importance? These and other similar questions had to be answered, always keeping in mind the main purpose of this Anthology and constantly trying to achieve a reasonable balance between the aesthetic, pedagogic, and historic considerations on the one hand and the dictates of space limitations on the other.

The purpose of this Anthology is twofold: to present a comprehensive survey of the entire keyboard literature through works which are appealing and representative, without being too demanding from either a musical or technical point of view; and to furnish an academically sound and varied teaching and performing library. The grade level of the contents ranges from easy to advanced, with the bulk of the material falling well within the intermediate grades. We felt that this segment of the piano repertory can furnish the most suitable materials for our multi-purpose collections. For this reason, works demanding utmost musical maturity and technical virtuosity, such as the late Sonatas of Beethoven, the lengthier concert pieces of Schumann, Chopin, Liszt, and others were not included.

All selections are based on authentic sources and are in their original forms. Tempo, dynamic, and expression marks in small print or in parentheses are editorial additions and should be regarded as suggestions rather than rigid directions. In line with our aim to give the player an authentic as well as a practical edition, the less familiar ornamental signs, especially those of the English virginalists and the French clavecinists, were replaced by the equivalent and better known symbols of the German Baroque (J. S. Bach). There is a review of these ornamental signs and their execution on page 18 of our baroque volume.   To aid the performer in avoiding the often puzzling problems involved in the recognition and correct interpretation of *long appoggiaturas,* these signs have been written out in conventional notation throughout the baroque and classical volumes.

The main body of this Anthology is compiled from the music of the great masters. Included are not only their well-known repertory pieces, but also other of their representative works which are seldom found in similar collections. We have also included a number of relatively unknown, nonetheless delightful pieces by a few minor masters. These composers were perhaps not creative minds of the first magnitude but they did produce occasional works of striking beauty, especially in the smaller forms, and should be entitled to the measure of recognition offered by an anthology.

We hope to have succeeded in conveying the many factors, viewpoints and considerations which guided the selection of materials for these volumes. The final choices inevitably reflect, of course, the personal taste and didactic principles of the editor. It should be noted, however, that the process of compilation also included extensive consultations and discussions with many distinguished pianists and educators. To them, too numerous for individual mention, we express our heartfelt thanks and gratitude. In addition, we are deeply indebted to Mr. Eugene Weintraub, for his invaluable editorial help, to Mr. Herbert H. Wise, for his patience and wisdom in guiding this large publication project, and to Professor Louis L. Crowder, for his richly illuminating commentaries on the styles and performance practices of each period.

October 1970   DENES AGAY

CONTENTS

7 The Classical Period by Louis L. Crowder

233 Biographical Sketches of Composers

235 Glossary

Music

Bach, Johann Christian

16 Rondo from *Sonata Op. 5, No. 4*

Bach, Johann Christoph Friedrich

20 Menuet and Alternativo

Beethoven, Ludwig van

156 Bagatelle (E-flat major) Op. 33, No. 1

160 Bagatelle (G minor) Op. 119, No. 1

164 Bagatelle (C minor) Op. 119, No. 5

162 Bagatelle (G major) Op. 126, No. 5

152 Für Elise *(Klavierstück)*

172 Rondo in C major, Op. 51, No. 1

165 Six Variations on *"Nel cor più non mi sento"* by Paisello

180 Sonata in E major, Op. 14, No. 1

216 Sonata in G Major, Op. 49, No. 2

194 Sonate Pathétique, Op. 13

Benda, Jiri Antonin

22 Sonatina No. 23 (G minor)

Clementi, Muzio

132 Rondo-Valse

125 Sonatina in F major, Op. 36, No. 4

Cramer, Johann Baptist

140 Etude (B-flat major)

138 Etude (B-flat minor)

Diabelli, Antonio

150 Rondino

Dittersdorf, Karl Ditters von

58 English Dances (Two)

Dussek, Johann Ladislaus

134 Canzonetta

Hässler, Johann Wilhelm

60 Sonata No. 5 (F major) from *Six Easy Sonatas*

Haydn, (Franz) Joseph

24 German Dances (Two)

38 Menuetto con Variazioni from *Sonata in D major* (Hob: XVI:33)

26 Scherzo from *Sonata in F major* (Hob: XVI:9)

42 Sonata in D major (Hob: XVI:37)

27 Sonata in G major (Hob: XVI:27)

Hüllmandel, Nicolas Joseph

52 Un Poco Adagio from a *Sonata in D major*

Hummel, Johann Nepomuk

144 Album Leaf

142 Scherzo

Kuhlau, Friedrich

146 Allegro Burlesco from *Sonatina in A minor,* Op. 88, No. 3

Mozart, Wolfgang Amadeus

102 Adagio in B minor (K. 540)

106 Fantasia in D minor (K. 397)

68 Minuets (Two) (K. 315a-315c)

81 Rondo in D major (K. 485)

111 Sonata in B-flat major (K. 570)

70 Sonata in C major (Sonata Facile, K. 545)

88 Sonata in F major (K. 280)

Reichardt, Johann Friedrich

145 Scherzino

Türk, Daniel Gottlob

55 Larghetto Amoroso

56 Sonatina in G major

Weber, Karl Maria von

230 Andante con Variazioni, Op. 3

226 Ecossaises, (Three)

225 German Dance (C major)

228 Waltz (A major)

THE CLASSICAL PERIOD by Louis L. Crowder

Late in the evening of the third of July, 1778, Wolfgang Mozart wrote from Paris to his father in Salzburg:

> "Mon très cher Père!
>
> I have very sad and distressing news to give you, which is, indeed, the reason why I have been unable to reply sooner to your letter of June 11th. My dear mother is very ill. . . . For a long time now I have been hovering day and night between hope and fear—but I have resigned myself wholly to the will of God—and trust that you and my dear sister will do the same."

The fact is that Frau Maria Anna Mozart, his beloved mother and his companion on this trip to Paris, the only trip on which his father had not accompanied him, had just died. Later the same evening, after four pages more to his father about the progress of his work, particularly the Symphony K. 297 which had been performed two weeks earlier, he wrote another letter to a family friend, the Abbé Bullinger in Salzburg:

> "Most beloved friend! (for you alone)
>
> Mourn with me, my friend! This has been the saddest day of my life—I am writing at two o'clock in the morning. I have to tell you that my mother, my dear mother, is no more! . . . She was quite unconscious at the time of her death—her life flickered out like a candle. . . . I pressed her hand and spoke to her—but she did not see me, she did not hear me and all feeling was gone. . . . I beg of you therefore, most beloved friend, watch over my father for me and try to give him courage so that, when he hears the worst, he may not take it too hardly. I commend my sister to you also with all my heart. Go to them both at once, I implore you . . ."

So it was actually from the Abbé Bullinger on July 12 that Leopold Mozart learned of his wife's death. Some may ask how could Wolfgang have misled him and entrusted the matter to a friend? How could he have continued his letter with a sparkling account of the relative trivialities of the preceding week? Was he perhaps a bit callous, or utterly self-centered and interested only in his work?

No assumption could be more false. Mozart was intensely devoted to his family and they to him. This rift in the circle involved days of tears for all of them, so any suggestion of insensitivity is unjust. His obvious desire was to give his father the comforting presence of a dear friend when he received the shocking news. And the remainder of the letter was not at all a contradiction nor an evasion of the sorrow which was to be with him for a long time. It served merely to make his temporary deception plausible, just as his deep concern for his father justified it.

The fact is that these letters reflect some of the attitudes of the true Classicist. It was simply inappropriate in Mozart's society to make public or even private display of grief beyond that which a restrained convention called for. Schubert would have written songs of stabbing intensity; Brahms did write a Requiem for his mother. Yet Mozart's symphony, written during his mother's illness and while he surely feared its outcome, is as sparkling as all his works of this period. Wherever there is tenderness, the mood is love, not grief. In fact there is absolutely no connection between Mozart's works at this time and the event that shook his entire future. If this reflects Classicism, how do we define it further?

The Nature Of Classicism

"Classical" music to today's teen-ager usually means *Clair de Lune* or perhaps *Malagueña. He* never mentions composers' names, for rarely does he know them. To his parents, who may have experienced some unavoidable contact with the arts, "classical" means anything not "popular," and this might include the *Grand Canyon Suite* or an abridged version of Rachmaninoff's *Second Concerto.*

At the other end of the spectrum of definitions, "classic" to the classics scholar means the world of ancient Greece and Rome. Finally, to the Romans themselves, "classicus" implied superior achievement of enduring value. Somehow this basic implication has survived and one hears, justifiably, of Jazz Classics, Moving Picture Classics, and will hear, I am sure, Sargeant Pepper referred to as a Rock Classic. These definitions, however, leave out the musician's concept of Classic.

To us Classic has come to mean the music of a definite period, about 1750 to about 1820, with some latitude for "classical" attitudes which made their appearance as early as 1730 in the pre-classical music of Gluck and Bach's sons, and for lagging classical influence present till about 1850 in the imitative works of many a second-rate composer. Classic in the musician's meaning is a fairly recent term and grew from the gradual identification of the qualities to be found in Mozart's and Haydn's music—balance, serenity, timeless completeness, simplicity—as being somehow related to these same qualities already observed in the sculptures and temples of antiquity.

Strangely enough, although there was a conscious "classic revival" in the arts during the late 1700's, stemming from renewed interest in the neglected ruins which dotted Greece and Italy, the term itself was only later applied generally to music. One writer, Niemetschek, does refer in 1798 to Mozart's music as possessing the "classic" virtues of timelessness and the superb balancing of form and content that were even then considered the virtues of the Greeks. More often other labels were used and "classic" had other meanings. Palestrina, for example, was termed by one writer "gothic" in contrast to a "classic" Handel. And in the early 1800's, when Romanticism was at the beginning of its astonishing upsurge, and when all great music seemed "romantic" to the younger modernists, Haydn's works were once referred to as "romantic tone paintings." So it was to be somewhat later that "classicism" was generally in use in its present context.

Music In A Changing Society

The music of the classic period does, however, reflect the classic trends in thought and esthetics of the times, as well as their turmoil. The French Enlightenment of the 1700's was an age of philosophers unequalled since the Greeks, and ideas of "reason" and "moderation" were cornerstones of their thought. The firm grip of clerical authority had been broken and heretical ideas were spreading far and wide. Both Voltaire and Rousseau, though intellectual opponents, had prepared the way for the French Revolution and the Rights of Man. Even the Archbishop Colloredo, Mozart's *bête noire,* was a fervent admirer of Rousseau. Freedom, for centuries a matter of individual revolt, had become a political and philosophical ideal for the first time since the Greeks.

Thus in spite of seeming tranquility, the music of Haydn, Mozart and Beethoven was part of a complete reorientation of values. The musician's patron had been for some time no longer exclusively the church, but increasingly the nobility. Soon patronage would shift to the rising and even more powerful middle class, the bankers and merchants. Moreover a general public was developing, and already music was being composed and performed for that nameless monster, the audience. In Italy the mass audience for opera had for some time helped determine its course of development. Performances on the piano began their slow but accelerating advance in popularity, even though a full evening of piano music was still unheard of. Mozart himself, after a childhood of performances in the salons of the nobility, gave "academies" (i.e., concerts) in the hope of attracting a larger public and making a profit.

At the same time, the amateur performer was becoming a musical force. Previously kings and emperors—Frederick the Great and the Emperor Joseph II were notable examples—had on occasion been excellent musicians. Now the wealthy bourgeoisie included in similar fashion, particularly in Vienna, a growing number of able performers and many others of more modest attainments, all of whom influenced the course of composition as works came to be written specifically to meet their needs. C. P. E. Bach, for example, entitled some of his works as suitable for "Kenner und Liebhaber"—connoisseurs and amateurs.

Beyond these pleasant innovations in music, the period was, in its political and social aspects, more explosive than any since the downfall of Rome. The French Revolution, which began in Mozart's lifetime, left a Europe that would never be the same again. The American Revolution stirred man's aspirations and offered a door of escape from serfdom. The entire world outside Europe became colonialized.

All this is to some extent gently suggested even in Mozart's music—the revolutionary libretto of Figaro, the veiled anti-clericalism of the Magic Flute, even the ominous presence of the Turks, who had missed by a hair's breadth dominating all of Eastern Europe but whose music fascinated Europeans. Yet, disregarding these international disturbances since they apparently had only slight influence on Mozart's intensely focused mind, it is impossible to detect any parallel between his personal life, his joys and sorrows, successes and disasters, and his music. Neither world events nor the "spirit of the times" nor daily vicissitudes were allowed to intrude on the true spirit of the times which demanded that the artist ignore them.

Here we have the very essence of musical Classicism. Not that the music of this period is not expressive, even personally and often poignantly so. It is simply that the viewpoint of the age was that music should be a universal, permanent expression, a "classic" expression, human but generalized. There are many instances of almost Beethoven-like intensity in the music of Mozart and Haydn yet never do they allow personal feeling to be identified. Never does this music become autobiographical. This is the undying strength of Classicism.

Unfortunately we are obliged to view the classical period from across a century of Romanticism, a century of the exploitation of the personal, in which no limits were placed on the public display of individual emotion. The romantic movement was as inevitable to the development of music as was the French Revolution in politics, and it did result in some of the greatest musical peaks yet scaled by man. Yet after the persistent melancholy of Rachmaninoff, the self-pity of Tschaikovsky, the exaggeration of Liszt—yes, even after the tenderness and torment of Chopin or the strength and exaltation of Schumann—what a joy it is to return to the serenity of Haydn and Mozart! Here our happiness is undying and our sorrows, discreetly hinted, become part of our human lot and are sublimated in music that liberates us from conflicting emotion and from all thought of our sins, mistakes, or griefs. The greatest music from the classical age will, like the greatest of Baroque, live far beyond the lifetime of all but the very best that has been composed since.

Other Characteristics Of The Classical Age

The Classical Age was truly international musically, even though national musical characteristics were becoming more of a preoccupation all the time. German and Italian musicians were everywhere, particularly in England and France. German composers wrote Polonaises, and the Austrian Mozart contributed the greatest of all Italian operas. The age of the traveling virtuoso was even foreshadowed in the wanderings of the Mozart family. And with greater mobility the status of the musician was rapidly changing. Though he was still officially a member of the servant class, the Rights of Man were having their effect. So while Haydn bore the humiliations of his station with patience and philosophical detachment, Mozart fumed and rebelled even though this may have meant financial privation. It would not be long until Beethoven could exist as one of the first of the great "free-lance" composers, in open contempt of social inequalities and even with occasional outbursts against a sympathetic and indulgent nobility. Beethoven had admired Napoleon as savior of the Revolution. Mozart, who was probably only dimly aware of what the Revolution was about, would have relished personal liberty as much as anyone, and had he lived another twenty years might even have written another "Eroica" symphony.

We have already mentioned the shift of the musical balance of power from the church to the nobility and finally to the upper bourgeoisie. The last step in this progression resulted in a spectacular growth in the performance of music in the home. The family string quartet became, especially in Austria, almost a universal institution. A generation later the piano, already rapidly supplanting the harpsichord in public and the clavichord in private, would emerge even more triumphant as the universal instrument. More suitable for private performance than the quartet since one, not four, performers sufficed, its day dawned brightly in the Classical age and reached high noon with Romanticism. Even today its twilight is not in sight.

Composition in general had to respond to these changing forces. Musical forms which had begun to evolve during the Baroque and which had gone through the adolescence of the pre-classical decades achieved polished perfection with the classical era, a perfection that has remained as the foundation for much composition even to our day.

The Sonata

Chief of these newly perfected forms was the classical Sonata, one of the great creations of the human mind. This abstract concept gave for the first time an adequate vehicle for the transmission of musical ideas of larger dimension than the dance types or fugues of the Baroque. No longer did a large composition depend on the stringing together of small sections as in the Toccata, or on words and plot as in Opera, but on the logical sequence and unity of the ideas themselves.

The Sonata achieved unity by limiting the number of ideas, usually contrasting in character, from which it was to be constructed. It permitted variety by the use of varying tonalities and by a free "development" section in which anything could happen as long as it had some relationship to the original materials.

The use of an essentially simple ABA structure to house all the manipulations the composer could devise was the fundamental stroke of genius upon which its entire evolution depended. The mind grasps readily the simple "exposition—development—recapitulation" sequence, delights in the unexpected and the ingenious which it meets within this basic simplicity, and, with the help of the unavoidable reiteration of the basic ideas, feels comfortably at home with them by the time the movement is over.

With Haydn and Mozart the sonata form became stabilized as the first movement of a three or four movement work, and proved so successful that it made possible the immense literature of keyboard sonatas, duo-sonatas, trios, string quartets, concerti, and symphonies. The literature of this form has continued to expand to the present day as each generation has contributed more "sonatas" in all these categories.

In fact so effective was the Sonata as a vehicle that the form tended, as the classic era declined, to assume more than its true function as a conveyance for musical thought and became something of an end in itself, a restrictive rather than a liberating influence. It needed the violence of Beethoven to crack its shell and twist its shape to accommodate the newer ideas of the romantic era—but that is a later story.

It is worth noting that, paradoxically, the classical period was largely without "classics" in the present-day sense of a list of time tested and beloved works which were included year after year in the performing repertoire. As in all preceding periods, practically all music performed was "contemporary," and usually the newer the better. One of the triumphs of the classic era was that works of its greatest composers were the first to become "classics" in our broader sense, and to achieve the distinction of being heard, enjoyed, and admired by every generation from their day to ours.

Hints On Performance

Music of the classical period, like that of the Baroque, needs in general a steady though not rigid tempo in order to convey its meanings. Indeed its expressive qualities evaporate the moment any romantic rubato intrudes. An Adagio of Mozart, for example, can be one of the most moving of musical experiences, yet any exaggeration in the sense of rhythmic distortion destroys both mood and meaning. Phrasings and shadings need the finest degree of subtlety; the very essence of good classical performance lies in expressive shading, and of course the graceful ending of a phrase often implies some slight "give" in tempo. But dwelling on a note in the manner of the uneducated tenor, or the push-on-hold-back style of the more naive Chopin players will ruin music of the period instantly.

Fortunately the matter of ornaments has been much simplified since the Baroque; many have disappeared and some are now written out by the composer. With the classical repertoire we are in a period when the old baroque rules were disintegrating, and the relative stability of notation habits of Beethoven's day had yet to be established. Trills, for example, were being liberated from baroque rigidity. Just how far the process had gone no one knows for certain. In many situations, cadences for example, trills still seem to demand an upper-note beginning, as in the Baroque. At other times they only sound convincing if begun on the principal note, as was to be the case a generation later with Beethoven. Instinct must be more of a guide here than in the Baroque, for the question whether Mozart followed strictly and all his life the rather pedantic rules set forth in his father's Violin School is not easily settled, as Dannreuther and others would have us believe, on the basis of a simple assumption that he must have done so.*

Appogiaturas have become simpler in that Haydn, Mozart, and later Beethoven usually wrote out the long appogiaturas, leaving a "short appogiatura" solution as the only possibility for those remaining, except in certain standard situations. These, as well as turns and other ambiguous notations, are clearly presented in our text. Fortunately we do not have to contend with the rhythmic uncertainties of the Baroque.

---

*For serious study of these problems, we recommend "Interpreting Mozart on the Keyboard" by Eva and Paul Badura-Skoda. This work includes suggestions for the solution of the more doubtful cases, and is helpful for all piano music of this period.

The piano technique of Classicism is joyously freed of the voice-leading restrictions of Baroque. Scales and arpeggios scamper about the keyboard; leaps and disconnected passages are no longer frowned upon. (Remember how Scarlatti's music had prophesied they wouldn't be?) Melody playing—usually in the upper voice, gives hints of the art it later became with Chopin.

Strangely, to our preconceptions at least, the "normal" manner of playing for most classical pianists and composers was a crisp non-legato, which of course contrasted effectively with the passages marked legato, which should, according to Mozart, be played as smoothly as oil. This attitude was reversed by the time of Beethoven, with whom legato playing was "normal" unless something else was called for. One can infer that he may have been influenced in this direction by Clementi, who, as a minority of one in the preceding generation, may possibly be considered the first classical champion of the "legato-as-a-rule" manner of playing.

Phrasing marks (slurs) to be found in most editings of classical music, including even the original editions, are not to be taken too literally. Often the bar line determined their beginnings or endings, rather than the obvious needs of musical thought. They should usually be considered as simply an indication that legato is in order. On the other hand, articulation marks, the short slurs or staccato marks within a phrase or motive, are generally carefully thought out and correctly indicated, and should therefore be observed.

Fortunately we have indications by the composer for tempo, mood, and general character. Not that they are plentiful or even adequate. One needs much more detail, particularly as concerns dynamics, in order to arrive at a complete interpretation. Either the student uses his own insight or accepts help from an editor. With this volume he may do either, for editorial markings are in small print and may be accepted or not as one chooses. A word of caution, however: to do one's own editing requires a considerable apprenticeship in playing this music. Over-confidence without this experience can lead to musical disaster.

A final word on the pedal: Does anyone need to be reminded that Mozart, after his childhood performances, and Haydn, in his more mature years, played the piano and not the harpsichord, and that all their mature works were written for the piano? Furthermore the piano of that day had the equivalent of the pedal, though it was operated by the knee. That Mozart used it freely is clear from his letters. However it is obvious that even his "free" pedalling must have been discreet, since over-pedalling is as destructive to good classical performance as excessive rubato. Mozart did not mark pedallings at all, Beethoven only erratically. Therefore only a developing taste and a keen ear can furnish solutions to pedalling problems, just as they must for matters of shading and tonal balance. Herein lies one of the main difficulties in classical music, and the reason why good performances are far from plentiful. Fortunately the ear develops as it is used, and taste creeps stealthily upward. Music of the classical period is the very best encouragement to both of these musicianly ripenings.

This Volume

The pieces offered in this, the second volume of the Anthology, were chosen to include both the familiar and the relatively unknown. In addition to the masterpieces of the three overtowering protagonists of the period, Haydn, Mozart and Beethoven, it is gratifying to find numerous charming works by a number of less familiar composers. We especially recommend Dussek's *Canzonetta,* Hüllmandel's *Un Poco Adagio,* Hummel's *Album Leaf,* Hassler's *Sonata* and the *Sonatinas* of Benda and Türk. The volume begins with the "gallant" classicism of Johann Christian Bach and ends with a generation of transitional figures, including Beethoven and Weber, whose early works reflect the classical tradition but whose creative needs lead them to a later and definitely romantic viewpoint.

Between the sometimes over-intellectual Baroque and the storms, fogs, tears, and struggle of the romantic era, the brief sunlit happiness of Classicism remains a perpetual joy to all who respond to its charm. A disarmingly simple facade masks the subtlest musical expression, asking nothing of us but to be enjoyed. This volume is a fitting introduction to this remarkable period and an inviting open door to savor its pleasures. It is our hope that it also may be an enticement to further exploration of this radiant era when good manners and kindness were not in opposition and when feelings were expressed with a restraint appropriate to one's reluctance to offend others.

Rondo

from Sonata Op. 5, No. 4

Johann Christian Bach

19

Menuet and Alternativo

Johann Christoph Friedrich Bach

Sonatina

G minor, No. 23

Jiri Antonin Benda

Andante un poco allegretto

Two German Dances

1

Moderato

Joseph Haydn

2

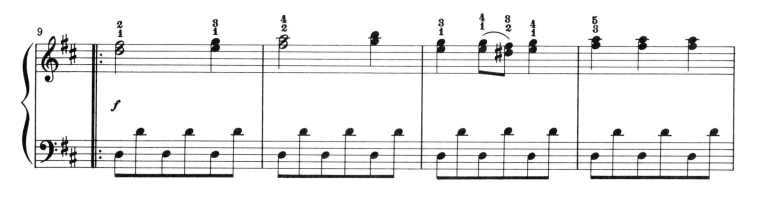

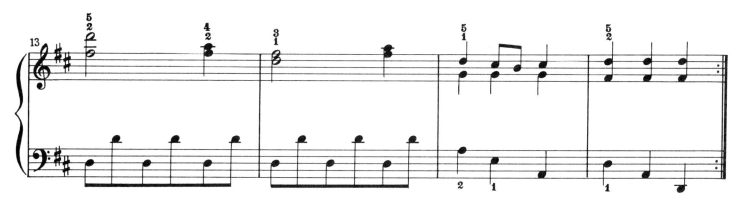

Scherzo

from Sonata in F major, Hob. XVI: 9

Joseph Haydn

Sonata

G major-Hob. XVI: 27

Joseph Haydn

Allegro con brio

Menuet

（Finale）
Presto

Menuetto con Variazioni

from Sonata in D major-Hob: XVI: 33

Joseph Haydn

Tempo di Menuetto

Sonata

D major · Hob. XVI: 37

Joseph Haydn

Allegro con brio

Largo e sostenuto

Attacca subito Finale

Finale
Presto ma non troppo

51

Un Poco Adagio

from a Sonata in D major

Nicolas Joseph Hüllmandel

54

Larghetto Amoroso

Daniel Gottlob Türk

Sonatina

Daniel Gottlob Türk

segue Finale

56

Finale
Allegro

Repeat Finale till sign (⊕),
then play Coda

⊕ **Coda**

Two English Dances

1

Karl Ditters von Dittersdorf

2

(*No. 1 may be repeated*)

Sonata

Johann Wilhelm Hässler

Allegretto con grazia

Adagio e sostenuto

Presto assai

Two Minuets

K.315/a - K.315/c

1

Allegretto con grazia

Wolfgang Amadeus Mozart

D.C. al Fine

2

Sonata

K. 545

Wolfgang Amadeus Mozart

73

Andante

Rondo Allegretto

Rondo

K. 485

Wolfgang Amadeus Mozart

84

Sonata

K. 280

Wolfgang Amadeus Mozart

93

Adagio

Adagio

K. 540

Wolfgang Amadeus Mozart

Fantasy

D minor, K.397

Wolfgang Amadeus Mozart

Sonata

K. 570

Wolfgang Amadeus Mozart

Allegretto

Sonatina

Op. 36, No. 4

Muzio Clementi

Andante con espressione

Rondo-Valse

Muzio Clementi

Canzonetta

Johann Ladislas Dussek

Etude

Johann Baptist Cramer

Etude

Johann Baptist Cramer

Scherzo

Johann Nepomuk Hummel

Album Leaf

Johann Nepomuk Hummel

Scherzino

Johann Friedrich Reichardt

Allegro Burlesco

from Sonatina Op. 88, No. 3

Friedrich Kuhlau

Rondino

Antonio Diabelli

150

Für Elise

Klavierstück

Ludwig van Beethoven

Bagatelle

Op. 33, No. 1

Ludwig van Beethoven

Andante grazioso, quasi allegretto

Bagatelle

Op. 119 No. 1

Ludwig van Beethoven

Allegretto

161

Bagatelle
Op. 126, No. 5

Ludwig van Beethoven

Quasi allegretto

Bagatelle
Op.119, No.5

Ludwig van Beethoven

Six Variations

on "Nel cor più non mi sento" by Paisiello

Ludwig van Beethoven

Var. 3

Var. 4

Var. 5

Var. 6

Rondo

Op. 51, No. 1

Ludwig van Beethoven

Sonata

Op. 14, No. 1

Ludwig van Beethoven

181

183

Allegretto

Maggiore

Allegretto da capo sin'al Maggiore,
e poi la Coda

Coda

RONDO
Allegro commodo

Sonate Pathétique
Op. 13

Ludwig van Beethoven

attacca subito il Allegro

Allegro di molto e con brio

Adagio cantabile

207

208

Sonata
Op. 49, No. 2

Ludwig van Beethoven

Tempo di Menuetto

German Dance

Carl Maria von Weber

Fine

Trio

dolce

D.C.

225

Three Ecossaises

1

Carl Maria von Weber

3

Comodo

Waltz

Carl Maria von Weber

Andante con Variazioni

Op. 3*

Carl Maria von Weber

*Originally written by Weber as a piano duet; transcriber unknown, possibly Weber himself.

Var. II *legato e con espressione*

legato

ben legato

Var. III

simile

BIOGRAPHICAL SKETCHES OF COMPOSERS

Bach, Johann Christian, b. 1735, Leipzig—d. 1782, London. Eleventh son of Johann Sebastian, a pupil of his older brother Carl Philipp Emanuel and, in his time, the most famous member of this great family. He is sometimes referred to as the "Milan Bach", through his years of service as organist in that city's cathedral. His most significant and productive years were spent in London. He was probably the first artist, in the year 1768, to give a piano recital in public and among the first to write piano music for four hands. A "modernist" by eighteenth century standards, he had strong influence on the young Mozart.

Bach, Johann Christoph Friedrich, b. 1732, Leipzig—d. 1795, Bückeburg. Ninth son of J. S. Bach; known as the "Bückeburg Bach", through his service as conductor at the court there. Although respected throughout Germany, he did not enjoy the international acclaim accorded to several of his brothers. Wrote a profusion of vocal and instrumental works which are, in style, close to Haydn's. He rightfully belongs among the earliest representatives of the classical period.

Beethoven, Ludwig van, b. 1770, Bonn, Germany—d. 1827, Vienna. A giant among composers. At the age of twenty-two he moved to Vienna, where for a while he studied with Haydn. His genius was quickly recognized and his fame spread throughout Europe. Began to lose his hearing around the age of thirty and eventually became totally deaf. His masterworks in all forms mark, during youth and maturity, the culmination of the classical era, and in his later years lead the way to Romanticism. His importance to music through two centuries has been incalculable. Particularly significant are the path-breaking force and liberating influence he represents in the evolution of piano music.

Benda, Jiri Antonin, b. 1722, Stare Benatky, Bohemia—d. 1795, Kostritz, Saxony. A most eminent Czech musician of the eighteenth century. A friend of C. P. E. Bach. Especially noteworothy are his keyboard sonatinas with their intimate lyricism, harmonic originality, and folk-like simplicity.

Clementi, Muzio, b. 1752, Rome—d. 1832, Evesham, England. Internationally famous as pianist and composer; England was his lifelong home. Had considerable influence on piano construction. His innovations in piano action and in piano technique contributed much to modern virtuosity. In 1781 he appeared before Emperor Joseph II in a piano performance contest with W. A. Mozart; result inconclusive. His collection of études, "Gradus ad Parnassum", his sonatas and sonatinas are still integral parts of the piano study repertory.

Cramer, Johann Baptist, b. 1771, Mannheim, Germany—d. 1858, London. Pupil of Clementi, to whose career Cramer's is an interesting parallel. Almost all his life was spent in England, and his activities included performance, composing, and publishing. He even composed études intended as preparation for those of his teacher. One of the more serious musicians in an age of virtuosity.

Diabelli, Antonio, b. 1781, near Salzburg—d. 1858, Vienna. Composer of many valuable, instructive pieces for piano students. He was also a music publisher and as such had lasting significance in the dissemination of the music of many great composers. A waltz of his served as the theme for Beethoven's masterful thirty-three "Diabelli Variations".

Dittersdorf, Karl Ditters von, b. 1739, Vienna—d. 1799, Neuhof. Friend of Haydn. A prolific, inventive and very popular composer during the second half of the eighteenth century.

Dussek, Johann Ladislaus, b. 1760, Czaslow, Bohemia—d. 1812, near Paris. A foremost musical personality of the classical period, eminent both as composer and as pianist. One of the earliest of the traveling virtuosi.

Hässler, Johann Wilhelm, b. 1747, Erfurt, Germany—d. 1822, Moscow. His charming, effective piano sonatas occupy an important middle ground between C. P. E. Bach and the mature classicism of Haydn and Mozart.

Haydn, Franz Joseph, b. 1732, Rohrau, Austria—d. 1809, Vienna, during the occupation by Napoleon's troops. Shared, with his younger friend Mozart, the greatest international musical fame of the eighteenth century. A supremely versatile and prolific master, he influenced greatly the development of the Symphony, the String Quartet and the sonata form, in general.

Hüllmandel, Nicolas Joseph, b. 1751, Strassbourg, France—d. 1823, Paris. Pupil of C. P. E. Bach; well-known pianist and composer of his time. Lived in London, Paris and traveled a great deal. Mozart regarded his piano sonatas as "very fine."

Hummel, Johann Nepomuk, b. 1778, Pressburg, Hungary—d. 1837, Weimar. Pupil of Mozart, Haydn and Clementi and teacher of Czerny, Hiller, and Henselt. Most famous of the early virtuosi. Contributed many new ideas on fingering and technique.

Kuhlau, Friedrich, b. 1786, Hanover—d. 1832, Copenhagen. Fled to Denmark as a young man to escape German military service and became, mostly through his operas, a pioneer of the romantic movement in Scandinavia. His solidly constructed melodious piano sonatinas proved to be of lasting value and are still part of the student repertory.

Mozart, Wolfgang Amadeus, b. 1756, Salzburg, Austria—d. 1791, Vienna. A true genius, perhaps unequalled in the entire history of music. Wrote his first composition, a little minuet, at the age of five; was ten years old when he wrote his first oratorio, and at fourteen he conducted one of his operas in Milan. Composed imperishable masterworks in all media: opera, symphony, church, and chamber music, sonatas and concerti for various solo instruments. Died at the age of thirty-five, leaving a musical heritage of unique beauty and classic perfection.

Reichardt, Johann Friedrich, b. 1752, Königsberg, Prussia—d.1814, Halle. At the age of twenty-four he became conductor at the court of Frederick the Great of Prussia. Was dismissed because of his known sympathy for the French Revolution. A sensitive, versatile composer; wrote much on music.

Türk, Daniel Gottlob, b. 1756, Chemnitz, Germany—d. 1813, Halle. Composer and writer on music; a theorist of considerable influence. One of the first to write children's instructive piano pieces, many still in use.

Weber, Karl Maria von, b. 1786, Lübeck—d. 1826, London. A transitional composer whose music retains many of the traits of classicism, yet whose imagination and individuality had much influence on later romantic composers. In opera, his most important field, one may discern most of the characteristics of romanticism. Wide interests — theory, music criticism, much writing on musical subjects, including the preparation of a musical dictionary.

GLOSSARY

Alternativo In 18th century instrumental music the term has the same meaning as the *Trio* of a Minuet or Scherzo.

Bagatelle A short, light piece, usually written for the piano. In this sense, the term was first used by Beethoven.

Canzonetta Literally, "a little song". An instrumental piece suggesting the mood and character of an Italian air or folk tune.

Ecossaise Although the word means "Scottish" in French, this dance probably did not originate in Scotland, but was born in the ballrooms of Paris during the late 18th century. Similarly to the *Contredanse* and *English Dance*, it is in lively 2/4 time and it usually consists of two eight-bar sections, each repeated.

English Dance, Anglaise Generic name for various lively dance forms of the 18th century, supposedly emulating the character of English country dances. The meaning of the term is very close to the *Contredanse* and *Ecossaise*.

Etude An instrumental piece, usually built on a single figure or motive, designed to develop the player's technical ability. Some composers of the 19th and 20th centuries, especially Chopin, were able to combine the didactic purpose of this genre with a truly meaningful and poetic musical substance.

Fantasia, Fantasy The term covers a wide variety of instrumental forms, all of which have in common a certain freedom of construction and often a quasi-improvisatory character.

"Für Elise" ("For Elise") Beethoven dedicated this piece to the daughter of his physician. The complete inscription, translated, reads: "For Elise, April 27, as a souvenir from L. v. Bthvn."

German Dance A term interchangeable with the Ländler. A type of country waltz in moderate 3/4 time, much cultivated by the Viennese Classics.

K. or K.V. An abbreviation of "Köchel" or "Köchel Verzeichnis", and, combined with a figure (K.545, for instance) a means of identification for Mozart's works. Ludwig von Köchel (1800-1877) made a catalogue of all of Mozart's works and numbered them in chronological order.

Minuet (Menuet) Graceful French dance in 3/4 time which became popular during the reign of Louis XIV mainly through the works of Lully. (The little Minuet by Lully in the first volume of this Anthology is one of the first examples of this form.) The dance retained its popularity all through the 17th and 18th centuries. Always in triple time, originally it was of moderate tempo, stately and refined in character; as such it became part of the baroque suite around 1700. In the second half of the 18th century, in a somewhat changed form, it was incorporated into the classical sonata and symphony. With Haydn and Mozart the tempo of the Minuet became livelier, its restraint and grace often replaced by a more robust, country dance quality, akin to the Ländler. With Beethoven the tempo further quickened and the form developed into the Scherzo.

Rondino A little Rondo.

Rondo (Rondeau) A musical form of French origin in which a main theme (rondeau) alternates with two or more secondary themes (couplets, episodes). Its simplest pattern is A-B-A-C-A, where A represents the main theme and B and C the episodes. The first great master of this form was Couperin. As the last movement of the classical sonata the rondo has a more rounded and cohesive construction. The favorite pattern of Mozart and Beethoven is A-B-A-C-A-B-A. There is smooth transition between the themes; the first episode (B) which appears in the dominant key, is repeated in the main key just before the last reprise of the main theme. The middle episode (C) is often replaced by a development section.

Scherzino A little Scherzo.

Scherzo The Italian word for joke, jest. A humorous, playful instrumental piece in 3/4 or 3/8 time. It is usually the third movement of a sonata, symphony or string quartet, and has the form structure of the Minuet from which it evolved. (Pattern A-B-A, Scherzo—Trio—Scherzo).

Sonata One of the most important of all instrumental forms. The name derives from the Italian word *sonare*, "to sound" on an instrument, in contrast to the Cantata, which comes from *cantare,* "to sing".

There are various types of baroque sonatas differing both in the number and the construction of the movements. The earliest examples of this form closely resemble the suite. In Kuhlau's Biblical Sonatas, the first keyboard works of the genre, each movement is headed by a descriptive programmatic title. Domenico Scarlatti's sonatas, true gems of the High-Baroque, consist of one movement in binary (two-section) form. In the sonatas of Pergolesi, Paradisi, Galuppi, and Kirnberger the polythematic character of the first movement and other architectural features of the later, full sonata are more and more discernible. The Clavier sonatas of C. P. E. Bach are in three movements, fast-slow-fast, and lead directly to Haydn, Mozart and the supreme master of the form, Beethoven.

The classical sonata usually consists of four movements: Allegro—Adagio or Andante—Minuet or Scherzo—Finale (Rondo). Occasionally the Minuet or the Adagio is omitted. The first movement is written in the sonata form, proper, often referred to as the Sonata Allegro form. This consists of three sections: *exposition, development* and *recapitulation*. The exposition introduces the main building blocks of the form, two or three contrasting themes, connected by transitory passages and ending in the dominant key (or in the parallel major, if the main theme is in a minor key). The development section further expands, develops these themes, or fragments thereof, in a great variety of ways. This section is usually very modulatory in character and tends to create a feeling of tension, leading to a climactic point. The recapitulation is basically a re-statement of the exposition, with certain changes to bring the movement to a close in the "home" key.

Sonatas of the romantic and contemporary literature tend to deviate from the above pattern. They are more free, and often more fantasy-like in construction, although in most cases they still retain certain elements, especially the architectural logic of this indestructible form.

Sonatina A short sonata of simple design. It may consist of one, two or three movements.

Trio Originally, a piece played by three instruments. Also, the middle section of a Minuet, Scherzo or other instrumental piece in ternary (A-B-A) form.

Valse (Waltz) The most popular dance of the 19th century and, in different stylized versions, a much cultivated instrumental form of romantic and even contemporary composers. Always in triple time, its tempo and mood can vary greatly.

Variations One of the earliest of extended instrumental forms, in which a musical thought (theme) is repeated a number of times, but always in a more or less modified version (variation). Each variation usually retains some melodic, harmonic or structural relationship to the theme. There are many different types of this form, from the *Chaconne* and *Passacaglia* of the Baroque to the more freely constructed variations of modern times.